The Montreal Piano School

Book 1

THE MONTREAL PIANO SCHOOL, BOOK 1

Copyright © Laird Stevens 2020

Published by Paris Press

ISBN 978-1-989454-18-3

PLEASE NOTE: TO RECEIVE A RECORDED COPY OF THE MUSIC IN THIS BOOK, SEND AN EMAIL TO:

MONTREALPIANOSCHOOLBOOK1@GMAIL.COM.

I WILL FORWARD YOU THE MUSIC SO THAT YOU CAN INSTALL IT ON YOUR COMPUTER.

A Note For Parents

If you already know the basics, that's great. You already know what your child is trying to learn and can help him or her with it.

If you don't know anything about music theory and you don't know how to play the piano, I strongly urge you to learn alongside your child. If your child can do it, you can too. The benefit is obvious: if your child gets stuck on something, you will be there to help. Otherwise your child may feel lost, and there is nothing that discourages learning so thoroughly as being lost.

This book is divided into two parts. First, there is the section called "Before We Start." It contains all the theory your child will need for many years to come. It is divided into lessons. Feel free to repeat a lesson—or go back to a lesson—as many times as you want.

The second section contains the music. Most pieces are one page long. Most are famous pieces. You child will probably know a few of them already.

Here is how I would recommend using this book. Sit at the piano and go through a lesson. Then listen to a few of the pieces on the net. Next time, ask if you child would like the lesson again, or would like to go on to the next lesson. Ask if he or she would like to hear the same pieces of music or would like to go on to some new ones.

I would also recommend that you play recorded music as often as possible so that you child becomes used to being immersed in it.

The basic idea behind my method of teaching piano is quite similar to the Suzuki method: it is easier, and more rewarding, to learn by listening. After children hear the music, they can hear if they are playing it correctly or making mistakes. They know how the music goes, and this guides them.

The basic difference between my method and the Suzuki method is that I teach theory at the same time as practice. This makes it easier to read music, and easier to learn new music on their own. I also offer advice on piano technique. Here it is.

Piano Technique Essentials

Many of the world's most famous pianists never practiced technical exercises. I would recommend against them. In the main, technical exercises are written by people who are not talented enough to write real music. The main problem with them is that they're boring, and boredom is the enemy of learning.

To master all technical difficulties (after Books 1 and 2 in this series), turn to Bach's two-part Inventions. These were in fact written as technical exercises, but Bach was a genius, and everything he wrote was beautiful.

Remember Chopin's dictum: the most important thing in playing the piano well is the fingering. (He also said the best fingering was the easiest fingering.) I have provided fingering throughout this book, but if your child finds better fingering, please allow that. Here, however, are some essentials.

1. Learn how to fold your thumb under your hand. The piano has eighty-eight keys, and you have only ten fingers. In order to go up and down the keyboard, you have to learn to fold under your thumb. To do this, place your hand flat and bend your thumb under it until it touches the back of the lowest joint of your little finger (or as close as possible). If it hurts, stop.
2. Practice jumping from one place on the piano to another. For instance, play a C+ chord with both hands and then jump each hand up an octave.
3. Learn to change fingers quickly on the same keys. Often, your hand position will be perfect for one bar and useless the next
4. Learn to change the sequence of your fingers from 1-2-3-4-5. For instance, in this example, you run out of fingers by the sixth note if you don't change the fingering:

C E D F E G F A G B A C B D C

1 3 2 4 3 5 HELP! I'm out of fingers!

C E D F E G F A G B A C B D C

1 3 2 4 1 3 2 4 1 3 2 4 1 3 2 AHH!

5. Always keep your wrist soft. If your wrist is stiff, you won't be able to play. This rule has some unfortunate consequences. Don't do anything that involves strengthening (that is, stiffening) your wrist. Forget tennis and hockey, for instance. But swimming and skating are good.
6. Here is a tip for very young learners. It sometimes helps, if the child is confused, to take his/her hand by the finger tips and press it gently onto the keys. Now, a child's fingers are very delicate. If you do this, you must place your thumb and second finger over the child's finger nail—the *lowest* part of the finger—and press gently. Never force. This is for guidance only. But if done correctly, it can have beneficial effects.

Reasons for Learning Music

There are many. Here's an academic one. Children who play an instrument are likely to do significantly better in tests at school. The articles I have read say that students do 5 to 15% better on their tests, and 15% is typical rather than uncommon. As well, this increased performance is seen in both girls and boys (equally) and in both language arts and math (equally).

Here's a second reason. Learning to play an instrument is a painless way to increase your child's self-esteem. Playing an instrument is something done in private, so no one can hear your mistakes, but you are witness to your own progress. There is no better way to build confidence.

But far and away the best reason to learn music is the enjoyment it brings. I am a pianist. I remember the day I brought my younger son home from the hospital. He was awake, so I played him some pieces on the piano. Now, this was a five-day old baby, but hear what I wrote in my diary:

> He was enchanted: he breathed in every note. If this was life, it was going to be very, very good.

And the amazing fact is that children will feel this way about music their entire lives. Music is a gift.

Finally, if you want to learn easily and maximize your enjoyment, listen every day. Listening is the key.

Table of contents

Before We Start	1
Jingle Bells (James Pierpont)	18
Lullaby (short version) (Laird Stevens)	19
Happy Birthday! (Patty and Mildred Hill)	20
Hush Little Baby (American folk song)	21
Land of Hope and Glory (Edward Elgar)	22
Für Elise (Ludwig van Beethoven)	23
Lullaby Op. 49, No.4 (Johannes Brahms)	25
Sonata 11 (Wolfgang Amadeus Mozart)	26
Early One Morning (English folk song)	27
Eine Kleine Nachtmusik (Wolfgang Amadeus Mozart)	28
Peter's Theme from Peter and the Wolf (Sergei Prokofiev)	29
Oh Dear, What Can the Matter Be? (English folk ballad)	31
Chorale from Cantata BWV 147 (Johann Sebastian Bach)	32
Silent Night (Franz Xavier Gruber) (easier version)	33
Silent Night (Franz Xavier Gruber) (harder version)	35
Rockabye Baby (English lullaby)	37
Busy (Laird Stevens)	38
Lullaby (complete version) (Laird Stevens)	40

The Montreal Piano School

Before We Start

You should read this at the piano with your parent or teacher. It's a sort of hands-on introduction to music and the piano.

LESSON 1: Octaves

What's an octave? An octave is eight notes. It's how far you have to go from one note until you get to the same note again. And it *is* the same note, but it's higher or lower.

A note is just a sound. All the keys on your piano keyboard give different notes. Imagine if they all gave the same note! Then you could have a piano with only one key. But you couldn't play anything interesting.

If you go to the keyboard and press a key, and then you count up eight keys, the eighth key is an octave away from the first key. But like I said, the two notes sound the same, only higher or lower.

The Names of the Notes

The notes all have names. They're just like the alphabet, only shorter. They start at A and end at G, and then they start over. A, B, C. D. E. F. G. This is painless. When you get to A again, you have reached the octave. Of course, if you start from B, and you get to B again, that's an octave too.

Let's find C.

There is no black key between B and C. However, there's also no black key between E and F. Look at the middle of the keyboard and find a white key that doesn't have a black key to its left. That's either a C or an F.

Notice how the black keys are grouped. First there are two together, and then there are three. The C is always below the group of *two* black keys. Find the C.

Now let's find the rest of the notes. Press the C and go down one note at a time. Remember you're counting backwards this time. C is the first note. The second is B, and the third is A. Note let's count up one note at a time. Just follow the alphabet: A, B, C, D, E, F, G . . . and then you get to A again. Doesn't the higher A sound like the lower one?

Now find C again. Find two white keys together. The C is right below the group of two black keys. Now hold the C down and follow the alphabet again. C, D, E, F, G . . . but then you have to start over. The note after G is A. Then it goes A, B, and C again. You've found another octave. Doesn't the second C sound like the first one?

That C you found is called *middle C.* It's in the middle of the piano, and you sit in the middle of the piano, so it's right in front of you.

LESSON 2: Intervals

The space between the notes is called an interval. An octave is an interval.

When you count an interval, you always start with number 1. Find C again. Now, instead of saying the alphabet, count the keys as you press them down.

C	D	E	F	G	A	B	C
1	2	3	4	5	6	7	8

The space between C and G is called a 5th. The space between C and F is called a 4th.

Now here is something interesting. Let's start at C and count up to F.

C	D	E	F
1	2	3	4

It's a 4th.

Now, let's start at F and count up to C again.

F	G	A	B	C
1	2	3	4	5

F to C is a 5th.

So a 5th is very similar to a 4th. If the C is *below* F (C to F), it's a 4th. If the C is *above* F (F to C), it's a 5th. It sounds confusing, but it's not really. You just have to count the notes.

Let's do another interval. Start at C and count up to E.

C   D   E

1   2   3

C to E is a 3rd. Now take both your hands. Press the C with your left hand and the E with your right. It doesn't matter which finger you use. Now play 3rds all the way up to the next C. Just keep your hands the same distance apart.

E   F   G   A   B   C   D   E

C   D   E   F   G   A   B   C

Now go back down.

E   D   C   B   A   G   F   E

C   B   A   G   F   E   D   C

You may find it confusing at first to say the alphabet backwards, but you'll get used to it.

Now let's do a 6th. Start at C and count up to A.

C   D   E   F   G   A

1   2   3   4   5   6

Now take both your hands again/ Press the C with your left hand and the A with your right. Now play 6ths all the way up to the next C. Again, just keep your hands the same distance apart.

A   B   C   Wait!

C   D   E

These sound just like 3rds. They're kind of upside down 3rds.

    C   D   E   are 3rds, but

    A   B   C

    A   B   C   are 6ths.

    C   D   E

Now play them up a whole octave.

    A   B   C   D   E   F   G   A

    C   D   E   F   G   A   B   C

You might like this better if you start with the left hand on the E.

    C   D   E   F   G   A   B   C

    E   F   G   A   B   C   D   E

There are only two more main intervals left to learn, the 2nd and the 7th. Here's a 2nd:

    D

    C

And here's a 7th (which is just an upside down 2nd):

    C

    D

Just for fun, play a whole octave of 2nds and a whole octave of 7ths.

    D   E   F   G   A   B   C   D

    C   D   E   F   G   A   B   C

It doesn't sound great. Now for the 7ths.

    B   C   D   E   F   G   A   B

    C   D   E   F   G   A   B   C

They don't sound much better. But 2nds and 7ths have their uses.

Find an F (it's right below the group of three black keys). Now play a 2nd:

    G

    F

Now, with your left hand, play this. Play the F six times.

    F   F   F   F   F   F

Now play the E six times (it's just to the left of the F).

    E   E   E   E   E   E

Now play the same thing, but add a G in the right hand.

    G   G   G   G   G   G   G   G   G   G   G   G

    F   F   F   F   F   F   E   E   E   E   E   E

Here's the rest. The right hand jumps up a 3rd and then a 2nd, and the left continues moving down a 2nd each time.

    B   B   B   B   B   B   C

    D   D   D   D   D   D   C

You know, most people never get further than "Chopsticks" on the piano, but you've already gotten there on your first try.

LESSON 3: The Black Keys (Sharps and Flats)

What about the black keys? They're not very complicated.

All the black keys are between the white keys. They're either higher or lower than the white keys.

They have special names. They're called sharps and flats.

If they're sharps, they're above the white keys. Sharps are higher. If they're flats, they're below. Flats are lower.

Now, every black key is above a white key, so why couldn't all; the black keys be sharps?

That's kind of like saying, why isn't every street just called a *street?* Why do there have to be avenues and boulevards and roads? They're all streets, really!

Absolutely. But sometimes the black keys are called sharps and sometimes they're called flats. That's the way it is.

The black key immediately to the right of C is called C sharp (usually written C♯). As you know, the white key to the right of C is D. The black key immediately to the left of D called D flat (usually written D♭).

C sharp and D flat are the same note, and you play them with the same key. (C♯ = D♭, if that helps.)

(Just so you know, C♯ and F♯ are usually called sharps, and E♭ and B♭ are usually called flats. G♯ and A♭ go by either name.)

So why are there sharps and flats? What are *they* for?

LESSON 4: Major and Minor, Scales and Chords

If you play a series of notes one at a time, without skipping any, you've played a *scale.* Here is the simplest scale there is:

   C   D   E   F   G   A   B   C

You can play it going up or going down. It's the same scale. It starts on a C, so it's called the scale of C.

If you play three notes together (or more than three, but let's start with three), you've played a chord. But you can't play *any* three notes. The basic chord is a note played together with its 3rd and its 5th. Here are some chords. Play them.

   G   A   B   C
   E   F   G   A
   C   D   E   F

Now, it doesn't matter how you arrange these notes. If

   G   is a chord,

   E

   C

then so is   and

         C   E

         G   C

         E   G

In fact, they're all the same chord. You should play these too.

This chord is called the chord of C major (usually written C+). The scale above is the scale of C major (C+). Now play this chord:

         A

         F

         D

It sounds different from C+. That is because it's a minor chord. It's called the chord of D minor (usually written D−).

If you play all the chords from the scale of C+, you will find three major chords and three minor ones. These are the major chords:

         G   C   D

         E   A   B

         C   F   G

These are the minor chords:

         A   B   E

         F   G   C

         D   E   A

(There is another chord starting on B, but we'll come back to that some other time.)

Play these chords and see if you can hear the difference between major and minor.

Now let's play a scale starting on G.

G   A   B   C   D   E   F   G

That doesn't sound quite right. It's fine until it gets to the F, and then it sounds funny. Play the scale of C again.

C   D   E   F   G   A   B   C

Now play the scale starting on G again.

G   A   B   C   D   E   F   G

It's the F. The F sounds wrong.

That's why there are sharps and flats. They are basically to make scales and chords sound the same as they do in C. So the scale of G major is this.

G   A   B   C   D   E   F♯   G

Play it. You'll see.

LESSON 5: Musical Keys

Most pieces of music are in a major key or a minor key. That depends on which scale is used in the piece. C major is the only major scale with no sharps and flats. All minor scales contain sharps or flats.

Here is the scale of A minor.

A B C D E F G♯ A

Oh, but you thought it was simple. It's not. That is called the *harmonic* minor of A. There is also a *melodic* minor, which has different scales going up and down. Here it is.

A B C D E F♯ G♯ A   That's going up.

A G♮ F♮ E D C B A   That's going down.

So what on earth does ♮ mean?

It's called a *natural.* It means *remove the sharp or the flat.* Basically it means *play the white key.* So you could write the descending scale like this:

A G F E D C B A

but you need to indicate that the G and the F are not sharped anymore when you're going down. That's why you add the ♮.

LESSON 6: Time Signatures and Key Signatures

Time signatures tell you how to count the time in a piece of music. Almost all music is written in 3 or 4 time. That means you can count it like this:

1 2 3 **1** 2 3,

or like this:

1 2 **3** 4 **1** 2 **3** 4

The *Star-Spangled Banner* in 3 time. *Jingle Bells* is in 4 time.

Music is divided into bars. A bar is just how many beats there are. In 3 time, a bar has three beats. In 4 time, it has four.

Often, a bar consists of quarter notes. In 4 time, this makes perfect sense. Each bar has four beats, and so each beat is a quarter of a bar long, or a quarter note.

Other notes are:

Whole notes	=	a whole bar long (4 quarter notes)
Half notes	=	half a bar long (2 quarter notes)
Eighth notes	=	an eighth of a bar long (½ quarter note)
Sixteenth notes	=	a sixteenth of a bar long (¼ quarter note)

Etc.

In 3 time, we stick to the 4 time words, because we don't want to have "third" notes. "Third" notes would be the same as quarter notes, and that would be *too* confusing.

Bars are separated by bar lines, vertical lines that go through both staves. At the end of a piece, there is a double bar line. Sometimes you will see a double bar line that has two dots in each staff. This is called a repeat bar line, and it means what it says. You should repeat the passage you've just played before going on with the piece. Repeat bar lines can come at the end of a piece (as in Brahms's Lullaby) or in the middle (as in Mozart's Sonata).

A time signature tells you how many beats there are in a bar. In 4 time, the most common time signatures are 2/4 and 4/4 (two or four quarter notes to the bar). In 3 time, the most common time signature is 3/4, but you can also find 3/8, 6/8, 9/8. 12/8, 6/4 and 3/2. It doesn't matter. What matters is that the eighth notes, or quarter notes, or half notes are always grouped in threes.

Then there are key signatures. These dimply indicate how many sharps or flats you have. The fact is: we all have different voices. Some people sing better in G and some sing better in C. When boys get older, they sing lower down. That's why there are different keys. In this book, I use only three key signatures, C+ (no sharps or flats), G+ (one sharp) and F+ (one flat). The exception is Peter's Theme which is in D+ (two sharps).

The key signature and the time signature are placed at the beginning of the first bar in a piece of music. After that, only the key signature is placed at the beginning of each line.

LESSON 7: Reading Music

Reading music is not easy, but it's not hard either.

Here is a tip. The easiest way to learn to read music is to know what the music already says. So listen to the pieces. Listen to them often. And then when it comes to reading the music, you will already know what the notes are saying. This will make it much easier to read.

In the meantime, the charts on the next few pages will help.

The Staves

Music is written on two sets of parallel lines called *staves.* If you're talking about *one* of them, it's called a *staff.* (Think *knife* and *knives* or *calf* and *calves.)*

For piano, there are always two staves, one for the right hand and one for the left. The staff for the right hand (the one on top) has a *treble clef,* and the staff for the left hand has a *bass clef.* The treble clef is meant to be a G—a very fancy G—and it circles around the line in the staff where the G is. (It's the G above middle C.)

The bass clef doesn't look even remotely like an F, but the two dots surround the line in the staff where the F is. (It's the F below middle C.)

Middle C doesn't fit on either staff. It's on the first ledger line below the treble staff and on the first ledger line above the bass staff. A ledger line is just a place to put a note that doesn't fit on the staff. It's like a tiny piece of the staff that goes on top of it or below it.

A note is written either on a line or in a space on the staff. Here is the scale of C+ written in both the treble clef and the bass clef.

Treble Clef

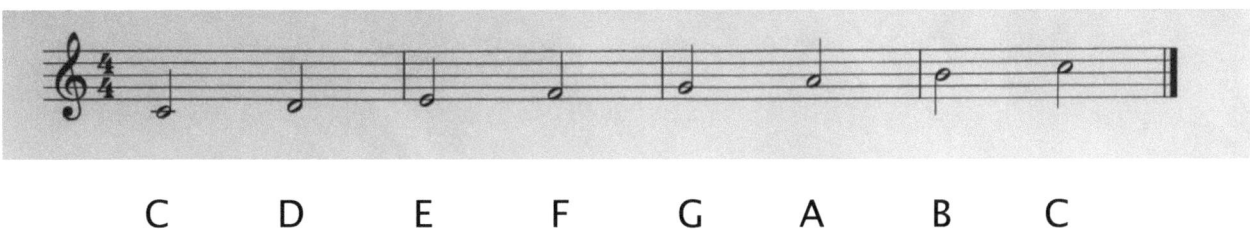

C　　D　　E　　F　　G　　A　　B　　C

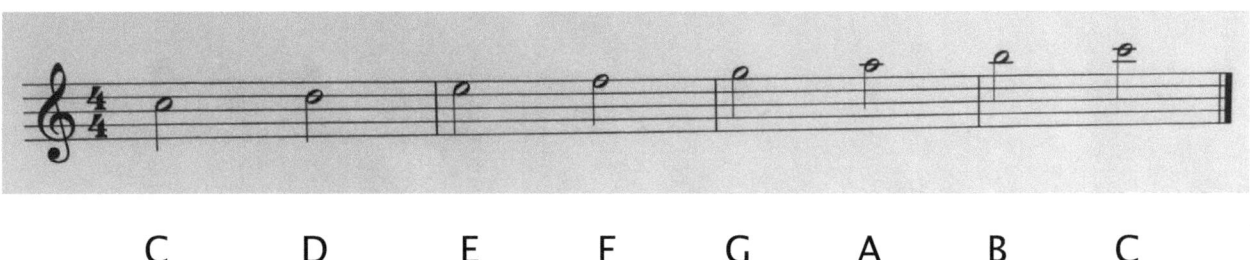

C　　D　　E　　F　　G　　A　　B　　C

Bass Clef

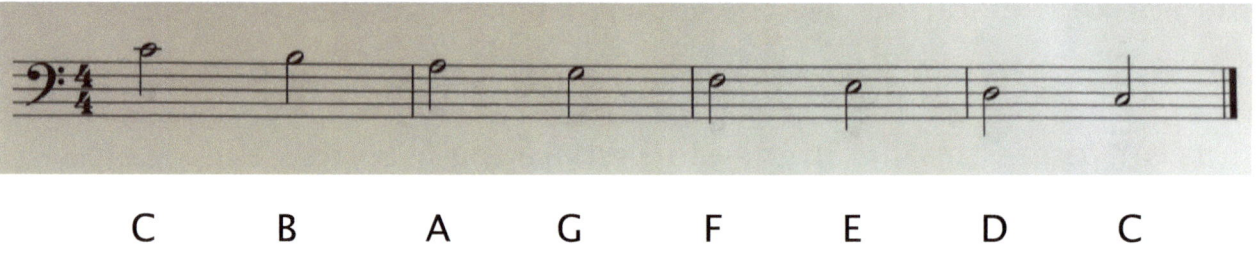

C   B   A   G   F   E   D   C

C   B   A   G   F   E   D   C

The Length of the Notes and Rests

A note sounds. A rest is silent.

The length of a note or a rest is determined by the bar it's in.

A note that lasts a whole bar is called a *whole note.* A rest that lasts a bar is called something uninteresting that you don't need to know.

Here is what the notes and rests look like.

Whole Notes

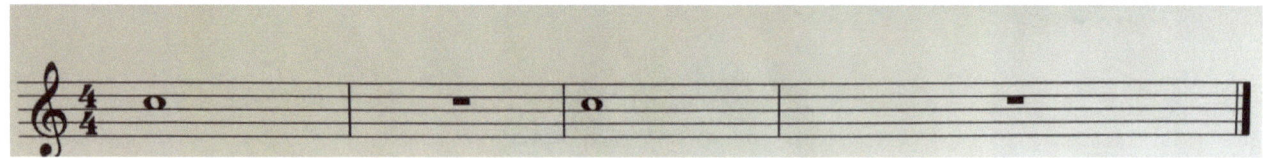

Half Notes

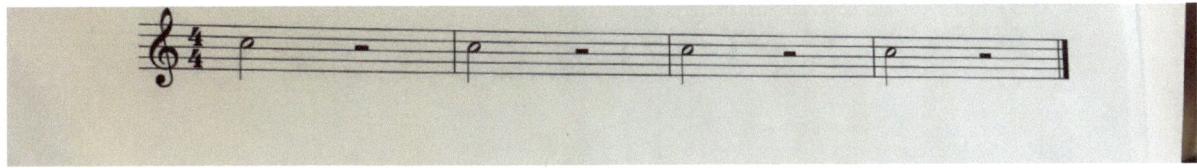

Quarter Notes

Eighth Notes

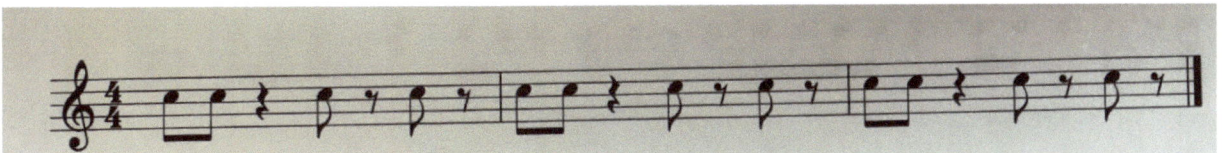

Sixteenth Notes

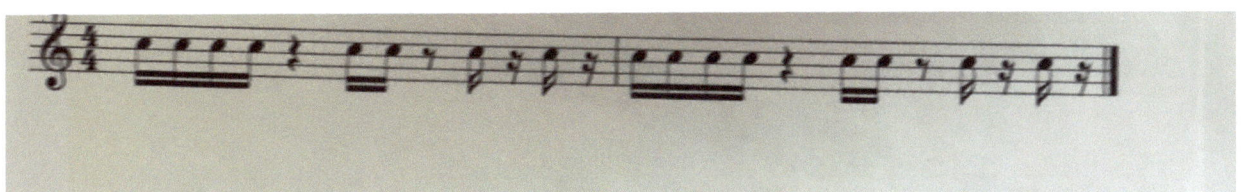

One last thing: if a note has dot beside it, then it's one and a half times as long as it normally is. A dotted quarter note is equal to a quarter note plus an eighth note, for instance,

And now it's time to look at some music.

Jingle Bells

Metronome 192

Janes Pierpont

Lullaby (short version)

Metronome 132

Laird Stevens

Happy Birthday!

Metronome 152

Patty and Mildred Hill

Hush Little Baby

Land of Hope and Glory

Metronme 96

Edward Elgar

Für Elise

Ludwig van Beethoven

Lullaby Op. 49 No. 4

Metronome 88

Johannes Brahms

Sonata 11 K. 331

Metronome 66

Wolfgang Amadeus Mozart

Early One Morning

Metronome 144

English folk song

Eine Kleine Nachtmusik

Metronme 126

Wolfgang Amadeus Mozart

Peter's Theme (from Peter and the Wolf)

Metronome 204

Sergei Prokofiev

Pages #29-30

Oh Dear, What Can the Matter Be?

Metronome 80

English folk ballad

Chorale from Cantata BWV 147

Metronme 96

Johann Sebastian Bach

Silent Night (easier version)

Metronome 80

Franz Xavier Gruber

Silent Night (harder version)

Metronome 80

Franz Xavier Gruber

Pages 35-36

Rockabye Baby

Metronome 88

English lullaby

Busy

Lullaby (complete version)

Metronome 120

Laird Stevens

www.ingramcontent.com/pod-product-compliance
Lightning Source LLC
Chambersburg PA
CBHW042014150426
43196CB00002B/43